D0555818

Searchlight
BOOKS™

How
Does Your
Body Work?

Your

Circulatory
System

Conrad J. Storad

Lerner Publications Company
Minneapolis

▶ To my beautiful, wonderful stepdaughters:
Sarah, the nurse, and Meghan, the teacher.
Thank you for all the love and kindness you
give to me and your mother.

Lerner Publications Company
A division of Lerner Publishing Group, Inc.
241 First Avenue North
Minneapolis, MN 55401 U.S.A.

Website address: www.lernerbooks.com

Library of Congress Cataloging-in-Publication Data

Storad, Conrad J.
    Your circulatory system / by Conrad J. Storad.
    p.   cm. — (Searchlight books™—How does your body work?)
    Includes index.
    ISBN 978–0–7613–7447–3 (lib. bdg. : alk. paper)
    1. Cardiovascular system—Juvenile literature. I. Title.
  QM178.S86 2013
  612.1—dc23   2011034264

Manufactured in the United States of America
1 – CG – 7/15/12

Contents

Chapter 1

PARTS WORKING TOGETHER

Each part of the body has a job. The parts work together. Parts that work together are called a system.

The body has many systems. One system helps the body turn food into energy. Another system helps the body breathe. Another helps the body to move.

The parts of your body work together. What are parts that work together called?

The Circulatory System

One important body system is called the circulatory system. This system's job is to pump blood to all parts of the body.

The circulatory system is made up of the heart, the blood, and many strong tubes called blood vessels. The heart makes the blood move through the blood vessels. Blood vessels carry the blood to all parts of the body.

Blood vessels are tubes that carry blood to all parts of the body.

Cells

All body parts are made of cells. Cells are so small you need a microscope to see them. The human body has many different kinds of cells. It has muscle cells and bone cells. It has skin cells and brain cells. It has nerve cells and blood cells.

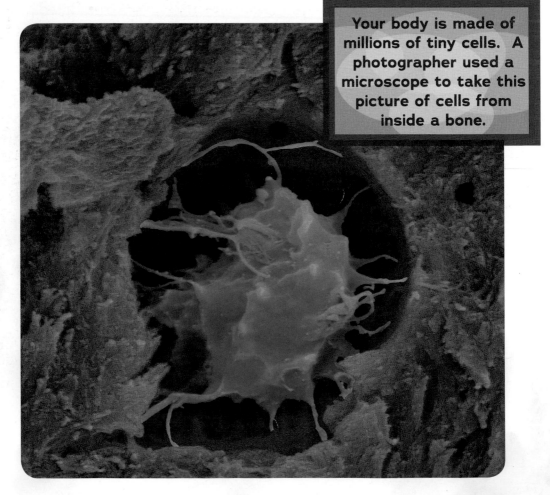

Your body is made of millions of tiny cells. A photographer used a microscope to take this picture of cells from inside a bone.

Every cell needs food to live. Food goes into the blood each time we eat or drink. Every cell also needs oxygen. Oxygen is a gas in the air. Oxygen goes into the blood every time we take a breath. The blood carries food and oxygen to every cell.

Your body breaks down everything you eat or drink. Then your blood carries the food to your cells.

Cells make waste as they do their jobs. The blood collects the waste and carries it away. Carbon dioxide is one kind of waste that cells make. Carbon dioxide is a kind of gas. The blood carries carbon dioxide from the cells to the lungs. We get rid of carbon dioxide every time we breathe out. Cells also make other kinds of waste. The body gets rid of these kinds of waste every time we go to the bathroom.

WHEN YOU BREATHE OUT, YOU GET RID OF CARBON DIOXIDE.

Chapter 2

THE HEART

The heart has a big job to do. The heart pumps blood to all parts of the body. It pumps blood every second. It pumps blood every day and every night.

The heart can pump blood because it is made of muscle. The muscles in your arms and legs make your bones move. The muscle in your heart squeezes to pump blood through your body.

Your heart never stops pumping blood. What is your heart made of?

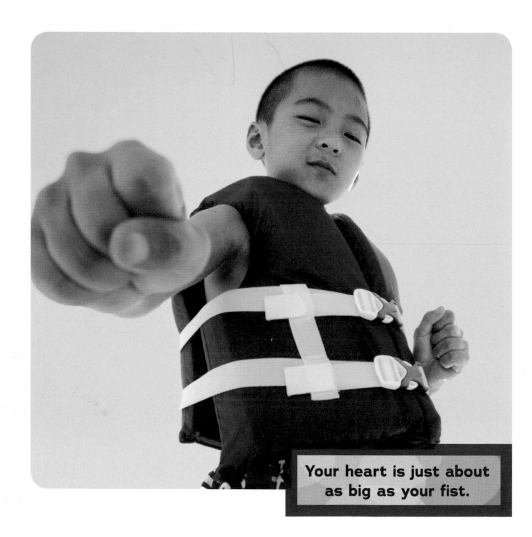

Your heart is just about
as big as your fist.

The heart works hard. But it is not very big. Your heart is about the same size as your fist.

The heart pumps blood when we eat. It pumps blood when we sleep. It pumps blood when we exercise. It never rests.

Your heart beats on its own. You don't have to think about making it pump blood. So you can think about other things, such as schoolwork.

The Septum

In the middle of the heart is a thick wall of muscle. This wall is called the septum. The septum separates the heart into a right half and a left half. The septum stops blood from leaking from one side of the heart to the other.

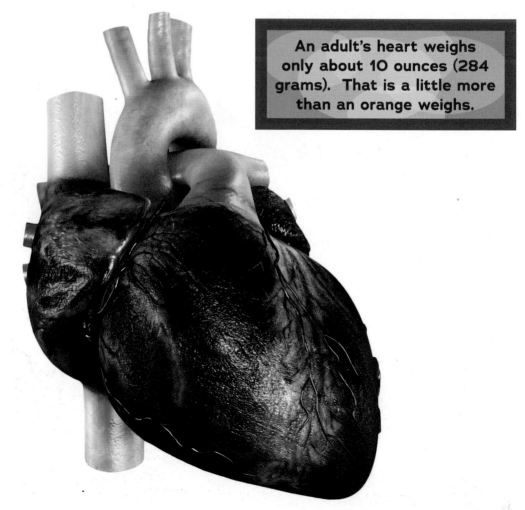

An adult's heart weighs only about 10 ounces (284 grams). That is a little more than an orange weighs.

Atriums and Ventricles

Each half of the heart is made up of two hollow rooms. The rooms are stacked one on top of the other. Each top room is called an atrium. There is a right atrium and a left atrium. Each bottom room is called a ventricle. There is a right ventricle and a left ventricle. As the heart pumps blood, the blood moves through each of these rooms.

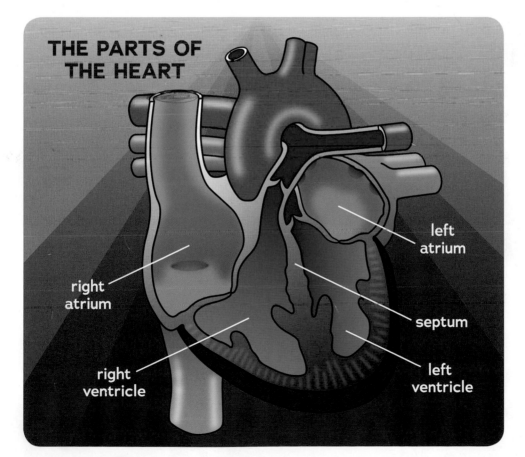

THE PARTS OF THE HEART

left atrium

right atrium

septum

right ventricle

left ventricle

13

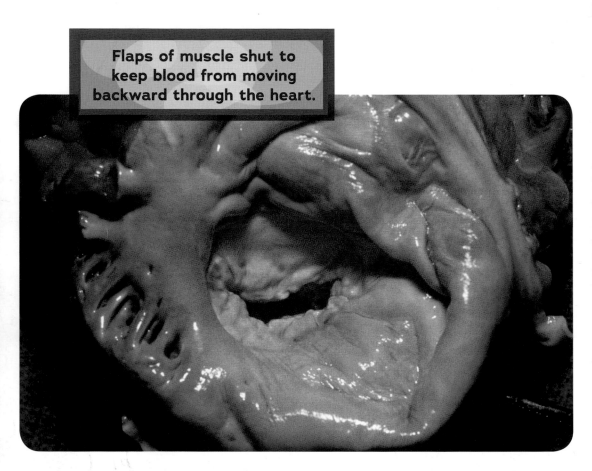

Flaps of muscle shut to keep blood from moving backward through the heart.

Blood always moves in the same direction through the heart. It moves from the left atrium into the left ventricle. It moves from the right atrium into the right ventricle. It cannot go backward.

Valves

Each half of the heart has special flaps made of muscle. The flaps separate the atrium from the ventricle. These flaps are called valves. Each valve is like a door. It opens only one way. When the valve opens, blood flows from the atrium to the ventricle. Then the valve closes quickly. It does not let the blood flow back into the atrium.

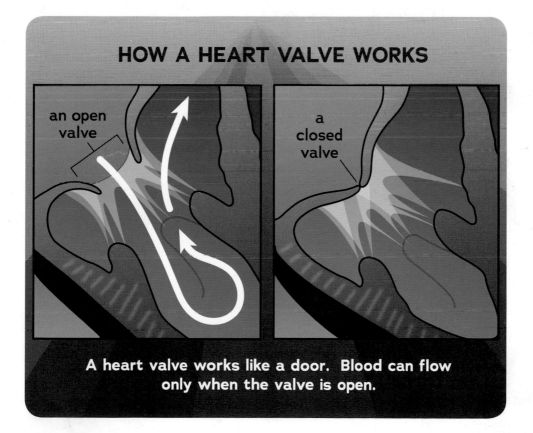

HOW A HEART VALVE WORKS

an open valve

a closed valve

A heart valve works like a door. Blood can flow only when the valve is open.

On the outside wall of each ventricle is another valve. When the ventricles are full of blood, these valves open. The blood flows from the ventricles into the blood vessels. Then the valves close again.

Doctors listen to the heart to make sure it is working well.

Heartbeat

The heart makes a sound each time its valves close. That sound is called a heartbeat. It sounds like *lub-DUB, lub-DUB, lub-DUB.*

Press your fingertips tightly against the inside of your wrist. Can you feel the blood pumping?

The heart beats over and over and over again. It always beats in the same way. First, the heart relaxes. Blood pours into the left atrium. This blood comes from the lungs. It carries lots of oxygen. At exactly the same time, blood fills the right atrium. This blood came from the body's cells. It does not have much oxygen.

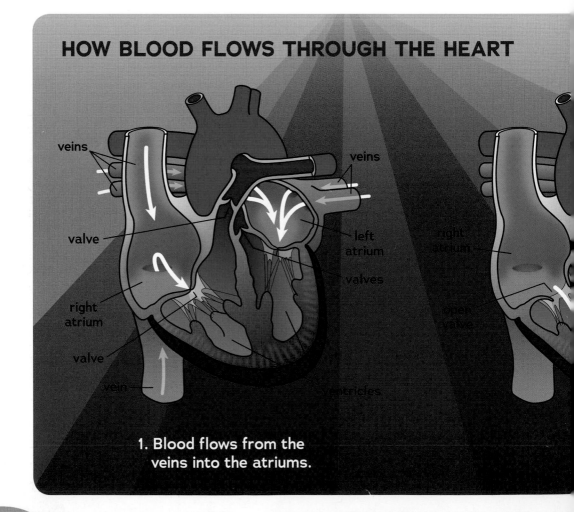

HOW BLOOD FLOWS THROUGH THE HEART

veins

veins

valve

left atrium

right atrium

right atrium

valves

valve

open valve

vein

ventricles

1. Blood flows from the veins into the atriums.

The valves inside the heart open. The heart muscle squeezes. Blood from the atriums is pushed down into the ventricles. The valves snap shut. *Lub*.

Next, the valves on the outside of the ventricles open. The heart muscle squeezes. Blood is pushed out of the ventricles and into the blood vessels. The valves snap shut. *DUB*.

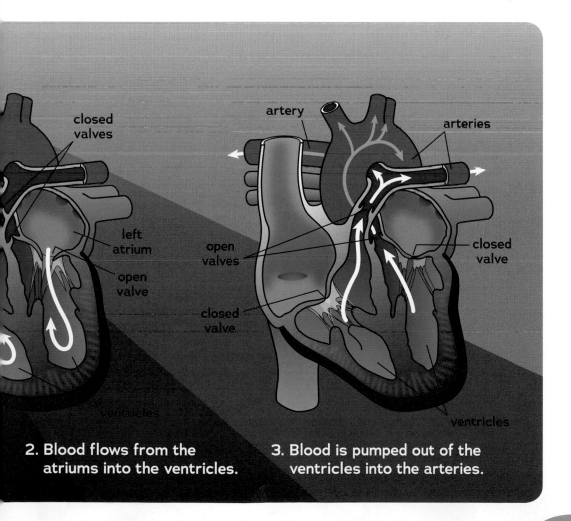

closed valves

left atrium

open valve

open valves

closed valve

artery

arteries

closed valve

ventricles

ventricles

2. Blood flows from the atriums into the ventricles.

3. Blood is pumped out of the ventricles into the arteries.

The right ventricle pushes blood to the lungs. There, the blood collects oxygen. Then it travels back toward the heart.

The left ventricle pushes blood out to all the rest of the body. It pumps blood to the top of our heads and to the tips of our toes.

Your heart is strong. It can pump blood high above your head.

Blood from the left ventricle carries lots of oxygen. The blood delivers the oxygen to the body's cells. Then the blood travels back to the heart. The right ventricle will pump it to the lungs to get more oxygen.

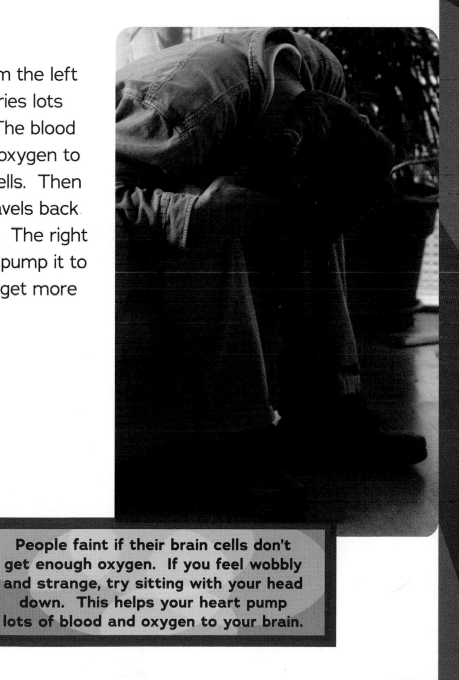

People faint if their brain cells don't get enough oxygen. If you feel wobbly and strange, try sitting with your head down. This helps your heart pump lots of blood and oxygen to your brain.

When a healthy adult sits still, the heart beats about seventy times each minute. But the heart beats faster when we run or jump. When we move around a lot, our body's cells have to work harder. When the cells work harder, they need more oxygen. Our heart beats faster to carry more oxygen to our cells.

Your heart beats fast when you run.

Your heart beats slowly when you are asleep.

The heart beats slower when we sleep. Our body's cells do not have to work as hard when we sleep. So they do not need as much oxygen.

The heart beats again and again. It beats every second. It beats every day and every night. *Lub-DUB. Lub-DUB. Lub-DUB.*

Chapter 3

BLOOD VESSELS

Blood is always moving through the body. The blood moves in two big circles. One circle runs from the heart to the lungs and back again. The other circle runs from the heart to the rest of the body and back to the heart.

The blood travels through the blood vessels. Some blood vessels are big. Others are tiny. There are three different kinds of blood vessels.

Blood vessels carry blood through the body. How many kinds of blood vessels are there?

Arteries

The strongest blood vessels are called arteries. Arteries have thick, strong walls. They carry blood away from the heart. Arteries carry blood to all parts of the body.

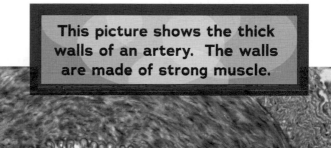

This picture shows the thick walls of an artery. The walls are made of strong muscle.

The biggest artery is called the aorta. An adult's aorta is almost as wide as a quarter. The aorta is connected to the left ventricle. Smaller arteries branch off of the aorta. As the blood travels farther and farther from the heart, the arteries get smaller and smaller.

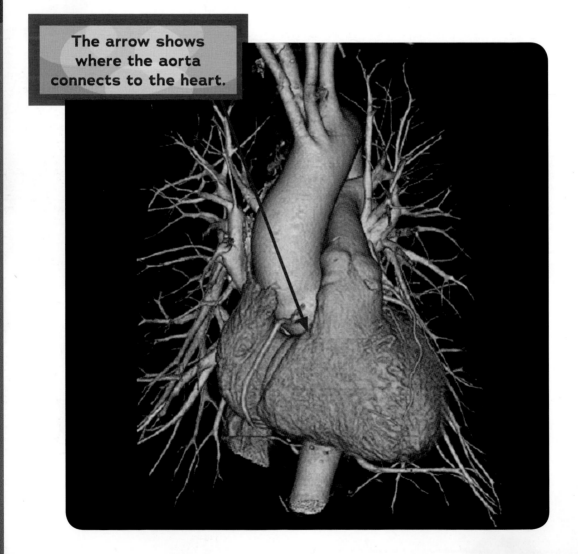

The arrow shows where the aorta connects to the heart.

Veins

Veins are the second kind of blood vessel. Veins have strong walls. But they are not as strong as arteries. Veins carry blood back to the heart. Blood in some of the veins carries waste from the cells. It does not have much oxygen. Other veins carry blood from the lungs. This blood has a lot of oxygen that is ready to be delivered to the cells.

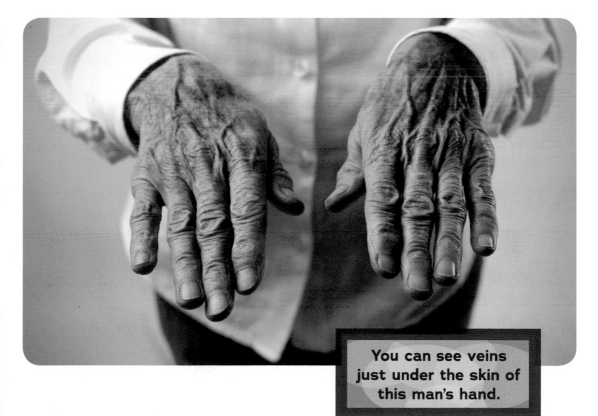

You can see veins just under the skin of this man's hand.

The body's biggest veins connect to the heart. Farther from the heart, veins are smaller.

An adult's biggest veins are about as wide as a pencil. These veins are attached to the heart's atriums. Veins that are farther away from the heart are smaller.

Capillaries

The smallest blood vessels are called capillaries. Capillaries connect the smallest arteries to the smallest veins. The capillaries are very important. They carry blood to every single cell in the body.

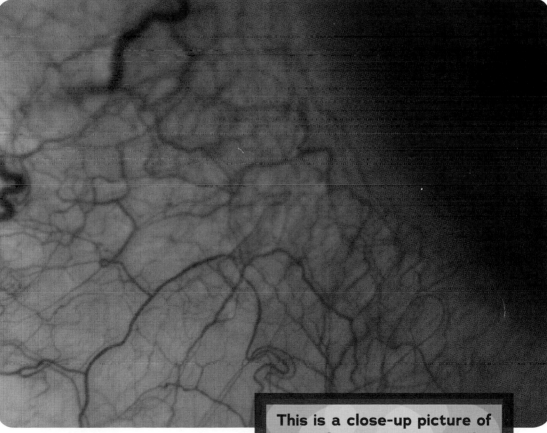

This is a close-up picture of part of a person's eye. The red lines are capillaries.

Capillaries are tiny. They have very thin walls. Food, oxygen, and waste can go right through the capillaries' thin walls. Food and oxygen go from the blood into the cells. The cells push waste out into the capillaries. The capillaries carry blood loaded with waste back to the veins so the body can get rid of it.

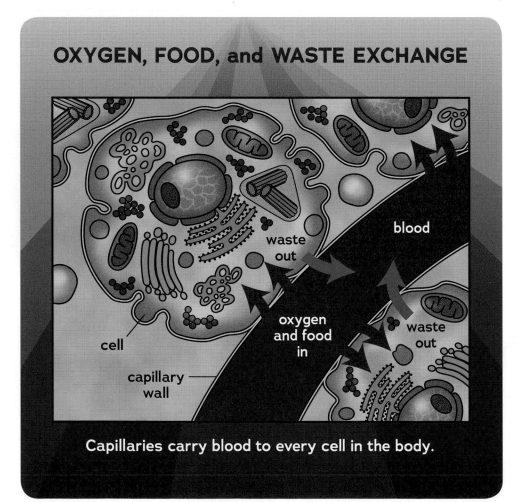

OXYGEN, FOOD, and WASTE EXCHANGE

blood

waste out

oxygen and food in

waste out

cell

capillary wall

Capillaries carry blood to every cell in the body.

A Repeat Trip

Blood travels through the body over and over. The blood flows from the heart into the arteries. The arteries carry the blood to the capillaries in all parts of the body. The blood flows from the capillaries into the veins. Then the veins carry the blood back to the heart. The blood takes this trip over and over again, every minute of every day.

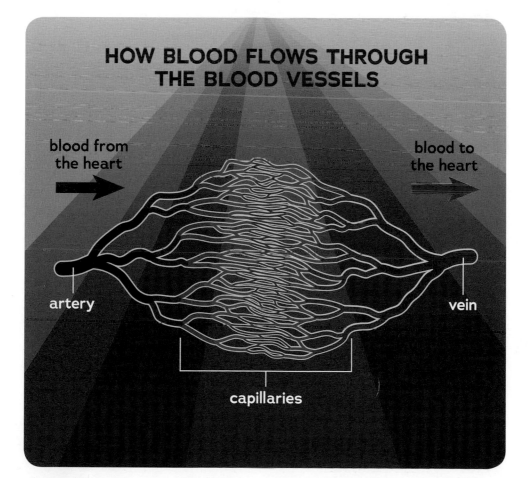

HOW BLOOD FLOWS THROUGH THE BLOOD VESSELS

blood from the heart

blood to the heart

artery

vein

capillaries

Chapter 4

THE BLOOD

Blood has lots of different parts. There are red blood cells, white blood cells, and platelets. All of these parts float in a clear liquid called plasma. Most of the cells floating in the plasma are red blood cells. That is why our blood is red.

A person who is sick or hurt may need more blood. Other people can help by sharing some of their blood. Why is blood red?

Red Blood Cells

Red blood cells look like flat, red doughnuts. Red blood cells contain a chemical called hemoglobin. Oxygen sticks to hemoglobin. Hemoglobin helps blood carry oxygen to the body's cells.

The body has millions of red blood cells. These cells live for only a short time. But the body is always making new red blood cells. Red blood cells are made inside of our bones.

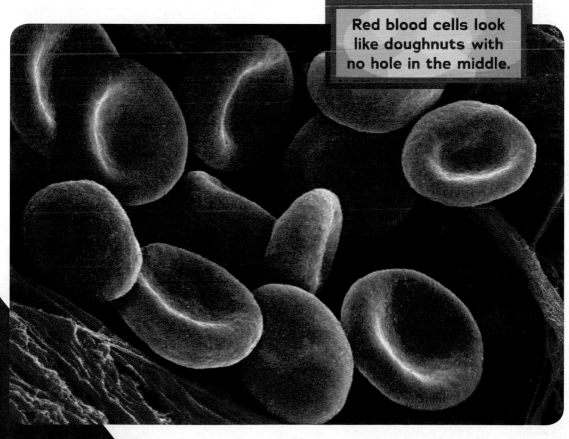

Red blood cells look like doughnuts with no hole in the middle.

White Blood Cells

There are not as many white blood cells as red blood cells. But white blood cells are still very important. White blood cells are like guards in the blood. They protect the body from things that might make us sick. White blood cells gobble up germs and other bad things that get into our blood.

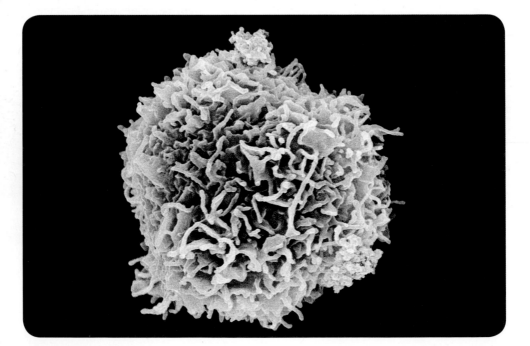

WHITE BLOOD CELLS LOOK LIKE BUMPY WHITE BALLS.

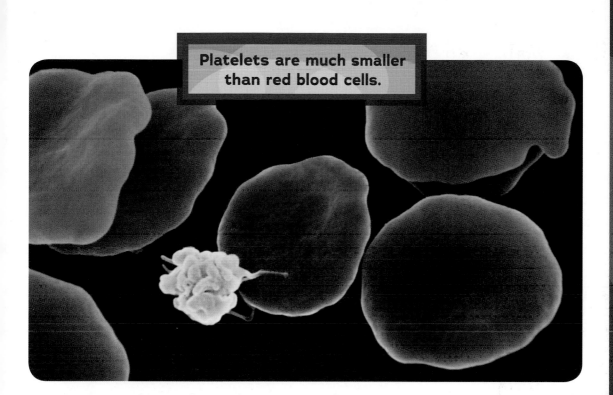

Platelets are much smaller than red blood cells.

Platelets

Blood also has tiny parts called platelets. Platelets help the body to fix itself.

If we get hurt, blood vessels may get cut or broken. Blood can leak out through a hole in a blood vessel. The hole has to be closed. Platelets in the blood stick to the edges of the hole. More and more platelets pile up in the hole. The platelets tell red blood cells to clump together over the hole. The cells form a hard clump called a clot. The clot plugs the hole and stops blood from flowing out through it.

Working Together

Blood is an important part of the circulatory system. But it is just one part. The blood needs the heart. The heart needs the blood vessels. All the parts work together to keep us alive.

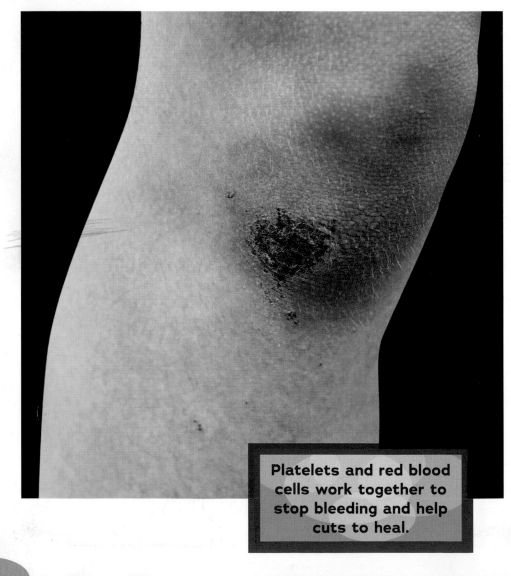

Platelets and red blood cells work together to stop bleeding and help cuts to heal.

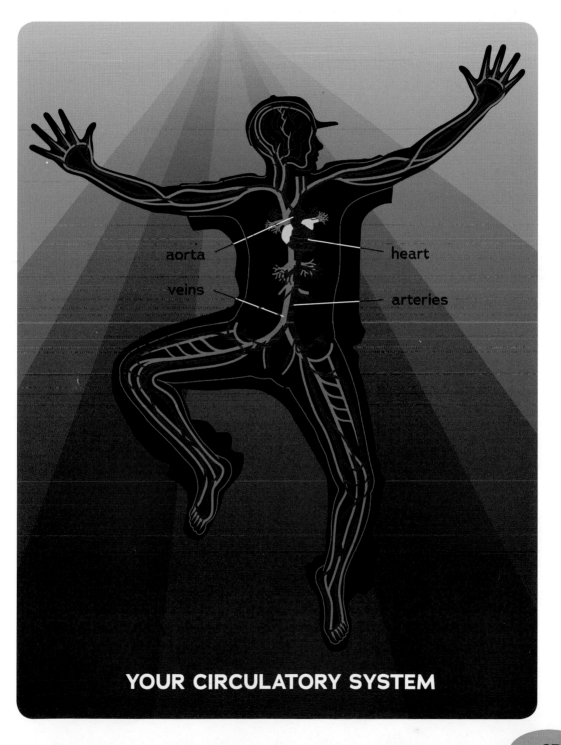

aorta

heart

veins

arteries

YOUR CIRCULATORY SYSTEM

Glossary

artery: a tube that carries blood away from the heart

atrium: one of the top rooms in the heart

blood: the red liquid that the heart pumps through the body

blood vessel: a tube in the body through which blood flows

capillary: a tiny blood vessel that connects the smallest arteries to the smallest veins

carbon dioxide: a gas that is one kind of waste that cells make

clot: a hard clump of platelets and red blood cells

hemoglobin: a chemical in red blood cells. Hemoglobin helps the blood carry oxygen to the body's cells.

oxygen: a gas in the air that cells need

plasma: the liquid part of blood. Blood cells and platelets float in the plasma.

platelet: a tiny part of the blood that helps the body to fix itself

red blood cell: a cell in the blood that carries oxygen. Red blood cells look like flat, red doughnuts.

valve: a flap of muscle that keeps blood from flowing backward through the heart

vein: a tube that carries blood toward the heart

ventricle: one of the bottom rooms in the heart

white blood cell: a cell that protects the body from things that might make us sick

Learn More about the Circulatory System

Books

Corcoran, Mary K. *The Circulatory Story.* Watertown, MA: Charlesbridge, 2010. Fun drawings and text make the circulatory system come alive.

Jango-Cohen, Judith. *Your Respiratory System.* Minneapolis: Lerner Publications Company, 2013. Read about another important body system—the respiratory system—and find out how it works together with your circulatory system to keep your body working well.

Lew, Kristi. *Clot & Scab: Gross Stuff about Your Scrapes, Bumps, and Bruises.* Minneapolis: Millbrook Press, 2010. Do you like to learn about the gross and funny side of science? Then you'll love this playful, gross-out look at blood, clotting, scabs, and more.

Taylor-Butler, Christine. *The Circulatory System.* New York: Children's Press, 2008. Find out how to keep your heart healthy and view diagrams, full-color photos, and a map of blood's route around your body.

Websites

Enchanted Learning: Label Heart Anatomy Diagram
http://www.enchantedlearning.com/subjects/anatomy/heart/labelinterior/label.shtml
This website features a diagram of the heart for you to label.

IMCPL Kids' Info Guide: Circulatory System
http://www.imcpl.org/kids/guides/health/circulatorysystem.html
This page from the Indianapolis Marion County Public Library has a list of resources you can use to learn more about the circulatory system.

KidsHealth: How the Body Works
http://kidshealth.org/kid/htbw/htbw_main_page.html
Click on the heart to watch a movie, read articles, and solve a word puzzle about this important body part.

Index

Photo Acknowledgments

The images in this book are used with the permission of: © Goldenkb/Dreamstime.com, p. 4; © Susumu Nishinaga/Photo Researchers, Inc., p. 5; © Dennis Kunkel Microscopy, Inc./ Visuals Unlimited, Inc., p. 6; © CanStock Photo Inc./jarenwicklund, p. 7; © iStockphoto.com/ Agnieszka Kirinicjanow, p. 8; © Monkeybusinessimages/Dreamstime.com, pp. 9, 20; © Joe Polillio/ Photographer's Choice/Getty Images, p. 10; © iStockphoto.com/Jeff Hathaway, p. 11; © Media-mation/Science Photo Library/Getty Images, p. 12; © Laura Westlund/Independent Picture Service, pp. 13, 15, 18-19, 30, 31, 37; © SIU/Visuals Unlimited, Inc., p. 14; © Asia Images/SuperStock, p. 16; © Ian West/Bubbles Photolibrary/Alamy, p. 17; Custom Medical Stock Photo/Newscom, p. 21; © iStockphoto.com/Kzenon, p. 22; © iStockphoto.com/Nicole Waring, p. 23; © Prof. P. Motta/Dept. of Anatomy/University "La Sapienza," Rome/Science Photo Library/Getty Images, p. 24; © CNRI/ Photo Researchers, Inc., p. 25; © BSIP/Photo Researchers, Inc., p. 26; © Bowie15/Dreamstime.com, p. 27; © CNRI/Science Photo Library/Getty Images, p. 28; © Lester V. Bergman/CORBIS, p. 29; © Wa Li/Dreamstime.com, p. 32; © Susumu Nishinaga/Science Photo Library/Getty Images, p. 33; © Steve Gschemeissner/Science Photo Library/Getty Images, p. 34; © Manfred P. Kage/ Photo Researchers, Inc., p. 35; © Tamara Bauer/Dreamstime.com, p. 36. Front cover: © Sebastian Kaulitzki/Dreamstime.com.

Main body text set in Adrianna Regular 14/20
Typeface provided by Chank